# The story of the lost sheep

Story by Penny Frank

Illustrated by Tony Morris

D0442908

THE LION
STORY BIBLE

42

TRING · BATAVIA · SYDNEY

The Bible tells us
how God sent his Son Jesus to show
us what God is like and how we can
belong to God's kingdom.

This is a story Jesus told to show
the people that they were all like lost
sheep until they came into God's
kingdom.

You can find this story in your
own Bible, in Luke's Gospel chapter 15.

Copyright © 1985 Lion Publishing

Published by
**Lion Publishing plc**
Icknield Way, Tring, Herts, England
ISBN 0 85648 767 8
**Lion Publishing Corporation**
1705 Hubbard Avenue, Batavia,
Illinois 60510, USA
ISBN 0 85648 767 8
**Albatross Books Pty Ltd**
PO Box 320, Sutherland, NSW 2232, Australia
ISBN 0 86760 552 9

First edition 1985
Reprinted 1986, 1987

Printed and bound in Hong Kong

**British Library Cataloguing in Publication Data**

Frank, Penny
  The lost sheep. – (The Lion Story Bible; 42)
  1. Lost sheep *(Parable)* – Juvenile literature
  I. Title
  226'.809505    BT378.L6

  ISBN 0-85648-767-8

**Library of Congress Cataloging in Publication Data**

Frank, Penny.
  The story of the lost sheep.
  (The Lion Story Bible; 42)
  1. Lost sheep (Parable)—Juvenile literature. [1. Lost sheep (Parable)
  2. Parables. 3. Bible stories—N.T.]
  I. Morris, Tony, ill. II. Title.
  III. Series: Frank, Penny. Lion Story Bible; 42.
  BT378.L6F73 1985    226'.809505
  84-26113
  ISBN 0-85648-767-8

One day, Jesus heard the teachers and
religious rulers grumbling.

'Jesus spends all his time with people
who are no good. Doesn't he know that
we are more important?'

Jesus looked at their proud faces and fine clothes. They did not listen carefully to what he said. They just tried to argue with him.

Then Jesus looked at the people sitting near him. Some were tired and hungry. Some had ragged clothes. No one else thought they were important. But they followed Jesus from town to town. They listened carefully to every word he said.

So Jesus said to the teachers and rulers, 'Listen to this story and try to understand.'

There was once a shepherd who kept his sheep up on the hills near the Lake of Galilee. He had been a shepherd all his life. He knew all there was to know about sheep.

The shepherd worked hard and his flock grew until he had one hundred healthy sheep.

He knew them all so well that he always noticed if one was limping, or had hurt itself.

One morning he was very worried. There was one sheep missing.

At first he thought he might have made a mistake. He counted again, very carefully, but sure enough there were only ninety-nine sheep in the fold.

'Now then,' said Jesus to the rulers.
'Do you think that shepherd said, "Oh,
never mind. That's too bad. At least
I still have ninety-nine"?

'Of course not! He left the ninety-
nine sheep in the sheepfold and set out
at once to look for the one that was
lost.'

That man was a good shepherd. He knew exactly which one of the sheep had wandered away. He would not rest until he found it.

The shepherd knew the hillsides very well. He knew all the places where a sheep might stray. He knew all the dangerous places where a sheep might fall.

The shepherd looked everywhere, even in places where he himself might get hurt. He must find his lost sheep.

At last the shepherd found his sheep,
up there on the hills.

He gently pulled it out from between
the rocks where it had been stuck. He
bandaged up the leg which had been
hurt.

Then the shepherd lifted the sheep up
onto his shoulders. It snuggled around
his neck and felt safe again.

The shepherd carefully made his way back. It was getting dark now, and he was hungry. He had been so busy looking for his lost sheep all day that he had not had time to eat.

The shepherd's feet were sore and
bruised from the rocks on the hillside.
But he did not mind. He was so pleased
he had found his sheep.

He put the poor, lost sheep in the fold
with the rest, and he counted them all
carefully.

'Ninety-seven, ninety-eight, ninety-
nine, one hundred!'

When he was sure they were all safe,
he made his way home.

As he walked along the dark street
he looked in at the doorways.

'I've found my sheep,' he called to
all his friends. 'Come and celebrate,
because I've found my sheep that was
lost.'

His friends and their families were very
pleased. They knew how important it
was to find that sheep. They all came to
celebrate with him.

'Can you understand?' Jesus asked the teachers and rulers. 'God's kingdom is like that flock of sheep. I am the good shepherd.

'There may be ninety-nine of you safely in the sheepfold, but I must search for the one who is lost.

'Even the angels in heaven celebrate when I find one of my sheep that was lost.

'I'm not like a part-time shepherd, who is paid to look after another man's sheep. That man doesn't really care if the sheep are safe, because they don't belong to him.

'I care about every one of my sheep.
I know them all by name. I always take
care of them. If one of them strays
I will search until I find it. I will
even give my life to save it.'

**The Lion Story Bible** is made up of 52 individual stories for young readers, building up an understanding of the Bible as one story — God's story — a story for all time and all people.

The New Testament section (numbers 31–52) covers the life and teaching of God's Son, Jesus. The stories are about the people he met, what he did and what he said. Almost all we know about the life of Jesus is recorded in the four Gospels — Matthew, Mark, Luke and John. The word gospel means 'good news'.
    The last four stories in this section are about the first Christians, who started to tell others the 'good news', as Jesus had commanded them — a story which continues today all over the world.

*The story of the lost sheep* comes from the New Testament, Luke's Gospel chapter 15. It is one of Jesus' best known stories. Luke follows it with the stories of the lost coin and the lost (or 'prodigal') son: all three show God's deep concern for everyone who strays away from him, and the lengths to which he goes to bring us back. There is joy in heaven over everyone who returns to God. Those who ask his forgiveness are welcomed with love. In John's Gospel chapter 10, Jesus describes himself as the Good Shepherd, who gives his life for the sheep. He comes to seek and save the lost.
    The next story in the series, number 43: *Come down, Zacchaeus!*, tells how Jesus brought new life to one of those 'lost sheep', Zacchaeus the tax man.